Soul Graffiti

What If Your Mother

— Or Father —

Was Wrong?

Michael-Renee Godfrey, RN, LPC

MICHAEL-RENEE GODFREY

Cover Art by Robert Williams

ISBN: 1497312159
ISBN-13: 978-1497312159

DEDICATION

This book is dedicated to my daughter and granddaughter.

CONTENTS

Note

This book is both autobiographical and hopefully, inspirational for you, the reader. In it I primarily relate experiences that emanated from my _mother_, because she was by far the greatest influence on my life. And, as a matter of convenience, when I held the mirror up to your life, I referred to your history with '_your mother_', as it would have been clumsy to regularly write: 'your mother or father.' It may very well be that your _father_ held greater sway over you. If that is the case, substitute 'father' for 'mother' as you read — I don't think this will in any way affect the journey that we will be taking together.

I tried my best to be brutally truthful in expressing all pertinent aspects of my personal experience, and I pray that my book helps to lighten your burden as it offers encouragement to truly love and accept yourself.

With the deepest respect,

Michael-Renee

ACKNOWLEDGMENTS

I thank God for giving me the vision to write this book. For, it is only by His grace that I have survived this thing called "life." I thank my parents for both the joys and the heartaches; because, in those moments that did not kill me, I only grew stronger. I thank my aunt and uncle, Joyce and Buck Godfrey, for always having kind words, listening ears, and compassionate hearts; but most of all, for always believing in me — no matter who else did or didn't. I thank my girlfriends, Lisa, Leah, Gwen, Niecy, Donna, Amani, and Alison for true friendship, honesty, and love — and for always encouraging me to live life however it presents itself and enjoy it as much as I can. I thank my girlfriend, Tracey, especially, for showing me how much power one question can have and for not letting me get away with the excuse of "fear." To my students at Shorter University — thank you for letting me know that "my story" and my unabashed willingness to share it helped you in some way. To LeighAnn and Arion — thank you for being a reflection of hope and healing in my life mirror and evidence of my purpose. To my girl Teshia — thank you for the simple, yet intense encouragement of "you have to write more…until the book is finished." To a very special person, James - thank you for everything - every compliment, every smile, every laugh, every ounce of motivation and for making me feel very, very special. To Kevin – thank you for introducing me to the best editor on the planet, Jack Barnard. To my editor, Jack – you wrote me once and said, "You don't have to do it alone, Honeybee;" that touched both my heart and soul and helped me get over my fears. Thank you. You mean more to me than you may ever know. To my therapist, Carla – thanks for listening every Monday at 5pm. Most importantly, I thank my daughter, Zari Sahar, for her "report cards" on my parenting and for using her voice; so that I at least had the opportunity to try to be a better parent and to learn to love her the way she needed to be loved.

~ Michael-Renee

i

1 *WORDS CANNOT BE TAKEN BACK*

"Renee, you are like used, dirty linen. Nobody
wants used, dirty linen."

Those are the words that I remember my mother
saying after she found out I was no longer a virgin.
I was 16 at the time, and trust me, the pastor had
been called. I had been punished and sent to my
room, awaiting some sort of exorcism. I remember
having a smart mouth and saying to my mother,
"So, what's gonna happen? Is my virginity going to
come back under my door while I'm locked in my
room?"

I probably shouldn't have said that; but that's what I
said because I knew my virginity was gone. I had
made that choice as a teenager. I had also made the
smart choice of getting on birth control; but none of
that seemed to matter — at least not to my mother.
I've wondered, for many years, how that affected
me; because, 28 years later, I still remember the

conversation practically verbatim. I remember sitting on my bedroom floor, and my mother looking directly in my eyes when she told me that.

So, from a mother to a child, that meant it was fact. At 16, I was "used, dirty linen that nobody was going to want."

I wonder if that's when I started to give up on myself?

I used to think that it started when I was 13; when my father walked out. My thinking was, "If my own father can walk away from me, then who would stay?" "If my own father doesn't love me, what person ever will?"

That, however, was only the beginning. I think I still had an opportunity to change, to be more, and to value myself. I don't know what it would have taken at the time — maybe therapy, a really strong mentor, or a mother who was emotionally available.

But, how could she be? She had her heart ripped out too. She was abused as a child. My father left her for another woman. She was broken; but I think my mother did the best she could as broken as she was.

No, I *know* my mother did the best that she could because we can only do as much as we know how to do. We can only be as emotionally available as we know how to be. And she didn't have good examples, herself, on how to be a good parent, how to be emotionally available, or how to be compassionate.

Unfortunately, for me, I think her comment became more of a self-fulfilling prophecy, because I am usually the type of person that will fight back — doing the opposite. If someone tells me that I can't; then I do it because I want to show them that I can.

But at 16, you don't really know what it means for someone to want you because of your value versus your sex appeal, your body, or simply because of a physical need that they need to fill for themselves. So, I guess, my quest became to show my mother that someone would want me; but it turned into more than just some ONE. It turned into promiscuity. Trying to find that one person, I guess, who would love me, who would stay, who didn't think that I was a "used piece of dirty linen."

I lost myself as a teenager. I wrote a lot of poetry about what is me and who am I. *Blue as the dove, white as the sky, what is me, and who am I?* I had no clue, no value. I felt like I had no purpose.

And I struggled.

I struggled with depression and low self-esteem. I was very bright and I made good grades; but for that, I was ridiculed at school. Academics were the only thing I had control over, really. I could control whether or not I got good grades. And in hindsight,

I guess I could have controlled sleeping around. For what? I was a "used piece of dirty linen that nobody was going to want" anyway.

Clean Slates

It amazes me how much power we have as parents. Dr. Phil once said that children are like clean slates and we as parents have the opportunity to write on the slate, which is our children's soul.

My Aunt Joyce taught me a long time ago that we always have choices in life. No matter what the situation is, there is always a choice in the matter. If someone is holding a gun to your head, for example, you have a choice. You can scream, pray, faint, wet yourself, fight, run, or do nothing. So, as parents, we have a choice about what we write on the clean slate of our children's souls. We have a choice to write something good and positive, despite the situation. Or we have the choice to write something demeaning and bad.

And sometimes — no, *all the time* — we are choosing to write something everlasting.

I have two cousins, Colin and Rashan, who always got positive things written on their souls by their parents; even when they did something bad, something of which their parents disapproved, or something by which their parents were disappointed. My Aunt Joyce and Uncle Buck always responded with something positive.

There were punishments. There were consequences. However, it was never because of whom Colin and Rashan were as people. Their parents were always clear that the punishment was because of the behavior, the act that was done; not because of who they were.

I remember, as teenagers, my cousin Rashan worked for me as a lifeguard. I was a pool manager at that time. And she did something that she knew would disappoint her mother. So, she came to me about it, asked my advice, and asked if I could help. And at first, I remember wanting to tell her, "Just keep it to yourself. Don't tell your mother." But that was because of my own experience and the fear of the consequences, which in my case would have been being berated, demeaned, punished, and yelled at — real negative things.

As I thought about it, however, in Rashan's case, it would be alright. So, I called my aunt and told her the situation — trying to prepare her for what Rashan was going to tell her — and I remember my aunt cried. But, I guess it gave her time to try to think it through and make her choice about how she was going to handle that with Rashan.

And it ended up being a very wonderful, bonding experience, I think, for the two of them because Rashan learned that she could trust her mother to not berate or demean her. And I think my aunt learned that, by being open to hear Rashan, Rashan would always come to her with the truth and with her concerns. They have always had a wonderful relationship where they can do that.

That's what I mean when I say we, as parents, have a choice about what we write on our children's souls.

Because of the teenage years I had with my mother, I didn't believe that I was going to make it. I tried to commit suicide at 16, 17, 18, and again at 23 because I never felt that I mattered. I just never felt that I mattered.

As a mother myself, I've tried to be very careful about what I write on my daughter's soul because I know how that can change who you are as a person. I know how much damage it can do and I also know how uplifting it can be.

Am I saying, because of those words that my mother said to me, that I have become nothing and nobody? Absolutely not. I have reached every goal I have set for myself in my life. I have gotten all the education I want. I have careers, as a registered nurse, a psychotherapist, and a sport psychologist, which I absolutely love. I have fabulous friends, a beautiful daughter, and a solid sense of self.

But, I know how I got there. I know how alone I felt. I know how much of a struggle it was for me. So, I try to say things to my daughter that will uplift her. I tell her how beautiful she is and how proud I am of her.

I am honest about my disappointment. However, even if I'm disappointed, it's always, "Zari, I'm disappointed because I know you can do better" or "because I know you know better." There is always something uplifting that I try to say. I don't just leave it as "I'm disappointed." I don't leave the implication that "you are a bad child" or "you are a bad person" because she's not. I try not to let my sadness, anger, or frustration fall down on her. Not to say that I haven't; because I have.

What I have learned, though, is that it is okay to go back and apologize when I know I was wrong — when I yelled and I shouldn't have or when I said something hurtful that I shouldn't have. Apologizing doesn't take my mistake away, but it lets my daughter know that I value her and I don't want to hurt her.

Do I think that my mother set out to maliciously hurt me? No I don't. Like I said before, I honestly believe my mother did the best she could. I believe her intentions were always good. They just didn't work out that way.

Are there mothers who vindictively and deliberately set out to hurt their children? Absolutely. As sad as that reality is, there are mothers who do it on purpose to break a child's spirit, to demean, and to degrade. I do not believe that my mother was that way.

But here's what it really comes down to: ***what if she was wrong***?

What if my mother was wrong? What if your mother was wrong? Just because your mother said it, that doesn't make it right or true.

When you finally figure this out, that's when life changes.

Had I known this earlier, perhaps my life would have been different. But, I believe that everything happens for a reason; and perhaps that was the way that God set things up, so that I would build strength and become the woman I am today.

 I don't really know. I do know that my mother was wrong — about me. I was not "used, dirty linen" that nobody would want. Somebody would want to love me one day. More importantly, I would want to love myself!

Abstinence makes the heart grow fonder
I found that out in the biggest way ever when I met my (now ex-) husband. I had finally reached a point in my life where I decided that I was worth more than I had been requiring of people. I was on a new faith walk. I've always had a personal relationship with Christ; but like a lot of Christians, I periodically strayed off the road. But I had come back to a place in my life where I finally allowed God to be in control and I submitted to His word.

I was trying very hard to be obedient and chaste, and a huge part of that obedience was to not fornicate. I thought maybe I would have to be single to make that happen and I was okay with that because it was very important to me that I lived God's word. Then, I met the man who would eventually become my husband. I told him that I was on this faith walk and it required a lot of me. I shared with him how I felt that I had been "used and abused," so to speak, by men; and was just deciding that I was worth more than that.

I told him that I would not be willing to have sex until we were married and I pretty much figured that would be the end of it all.

The first year of our relationship was long distance because he lived in New York and I lived in Georgia. We were both in the military and were being deployed back and forth to Iraq and Afghanistan; so, we kind of cruised through the first year because we couldn't really see each other.

But that second year came and a choice had to be made. I asked my then fiancé (he proposed two weeks after we met) if he would be willing to respect what I was trying to do. Not really if he would be willing — more like, "This is the way that it is. Are you willing to accept it or not?" I gave him some time to think about it; and when we breached the topic again, he looked me straight in the eye, and said five words to me that changed my entire life. They transformed who I felt I was as a woman and as a person. They confirmed my self-worth and world value.

What he said to me was, "You are worth the wait."

It was amazing!

To hear somebody say that about me — it was incredible how that changed me. Now, of course there was skepticism. I figured he was just saying what he needed to say to still get in my pants. I waited for him to try something anyway.

But, he didn't. That was the interesting thing. So, his actions backed up his words. He showed me that I was worth it. He validated what I wanted to believe for so long, and what I finally felt for myself.

It was absolutely, positively amazing.

My mother was wrong.

I finally figured that out. My mother was wrong. God proved that to me by helping me learn to believe in myself, by giving me a chance to do right by my daughter, and by positioning me to hear five words that confirmed His promise for me.

So, I suppose you are wondering: *Then, why is he your ex-husband?*

The answer is: Because he was a serial cheater and ended up having a baby with another woman; and I knew I deserved better than that. I knew that I was worth more than that. I knew that I had done right by him and had to make a choice for myself about how I was going to allow him to treat me.

I chose to get out of a situation that had, unfortunately, deteriorated; and give myself the opportunity to be loved the way I deserved to be loved.

Still, this doesn't belie the fact that his willingness, in the early part of our relationship, to accept my need to refrain from sex was a major part of healing the damage my mother had done.

> *"The only person who can pull me down is myself, and I'm not going to let myself pull me down anymore."*   C. JoyBell C.

Contemplation: How far back does your pain go? What is your earliest memory of questioning your worth? Are you ready to start healing? If you don't have one already, I encourage you to find a good therapist to help you process your feelings.

Now, make a commitment to yourself:
Today, I commit to start letting go of things that hold me back, getting to know myself, and learning to love myself in order to make me the best me I can be as defined by me.

Signature: _____

2 *SOUL GRAFFITI*

"Individuals are not born with a self-concept but develop it through interaction with others, particularly family members"
Cooley, 1902 as cited in Stone, 2009

Children come into this world with clean, pure souls. They learn to trust because they have no choice. They have not yet experienced disappointment. They look to their parents to teach them about right and wrong, hot and cold. They look to their parents to teach them how to be strong and stand up for the things in which they believe.

Our children's values, morals, and beliefs are based on what they see their parents do and what they hear their parents say. Children are not born racists. They are not born with low self-esteem. We, their parents, shape and mold a significant part of their personalities and help them determine who they believe they are.

Spray paint
Like the brick walls on which graffiti artists draw, our children's souls are open to us as blank slates. And as graffiti artists carefully consider what they will draw to express their feelings and mark their existence, we should carefully consider what we will write on the souls of our children. A graffiti artist who spray paints profanity on the wall will leave one impression; while, the artist who spray paints a mural that inspires hope and love will leave quite a different impression.

What did your mother, or father, spray paint on your wall that you continue to see every day — despite everything you have tried to hide it? Was it: "You can be anything you want to be" or "You will never amount to anything?"

You know, we run from both success and failure.

What have you written on the souls of your children that will stay with them forever? Is it: "My love for you is unconditional" or "I will only show you love when you are acting the way I think you should?"

Are your messages contradictory? For example, have you told your kids there is nothing they could ever to do to make you stop loving them and then turned around and stopped speaking to them because they interrupted your "date night" or they made a critical life mistake?

Have you told your daughter that you will always be there for her, yet you are never available when you are in a relationship?

Have you told your son that he is the man of the house, yet expect him to submit his "reign" to each of your new boyfriends?

Have you told your kids that you have to make time for what's important in life, but rarely put them on your "to do" list or act as though it is a burden when you finally do?

We have a choice about what we write on our children's souls. We can build them up or break them down. We can write good things or bad things — it's that simple.

But know this: whatever is written there will be *internalized* and *believed*.

Parents have the "artist's privilege" because parents are the first artists to draw on their children's canvases. Everyone who came after your parents, and everyone who comes after us, can only write over what was originally written there.

Everyone!

Contemplation: Get a pencil and paper – A PENCIL – and write down all the words that have been spray painted on your soul - good and bad. I am asking you to use a pencil so that as you go through this book, you can easily erase mistakes. That's how we should write our lives, in pencil vs. permanent marker; so, we can erase and make changes. Now, take a look at the list. Are all those words true? Are those words that *you* wrote there or are those words that *your mother* wrote there? Go through your list using the following symbols:

(abc)   Put a line through all the words written by someone else that are not true.

(?)   Put a question mark by those of which you are unsure.

(√)   Put a checkmark by the ones you know to be true.

Focus on the **positive** ones with the checkmarks for now. Write them on an index card and put them someplace you will see them every day. Repeat them to yourself throughout the day – until they feel genuine. We will deal with the other words later; so keep your list.

3 THE PAINT WE USE

*"All children behave as well as they are
treated."* Jan Hunt

So, what has your mother said to you that was
wrong?

What was the incorrect prophecy that you have
believed for so long?

*What is it that has held you back from meeting your
full potential?*

*Did she tell you that you were worthless, selfish,
stupid, fat, ugly, or deceitful?*

*Did your mother, in some way, cause you to believe
that you were forever
out of God's favor — never, ever to be redeemed?*

*Did she say something that made you feel you were
not worthy to be on this planet?*

Did she say something that caused you to question your value or purpose in life?

Stop and think back. You bought this book for a reason. Something about the title, perhaps, made you ask yourself, ***"What if she really was wrong?"***

So, what did your mother say to you that still clings to your soul and stops you from being the person that God intended?

I realize this is a hard journey to take. For years, you try to just forget the hurt, pain, and humiliation. You think you should feel satisfied because of your career success, your parenting success, your marital success, or simply by personal triumph; but somehow, you can't find joy.

There is an empty space that you still just cannot seem to fill. There are still unexplained doubts about yourself. There are still unsilenced whispers of your mother's words that are heard in your subconscious.

Every success comes with a sense of relief that you had not fulfilled your mother's prophecy. Or it comes with a sense of vindication, as if to say, "Now what do you have to say?" It *rarely* seems to come with just a quiet, peaceful feeling of accomplishment just because you knew you could. And it *very rarely* comes with a boisterous celebration of our accomplishment. That is actually a normal response for those of us who grew up with a mother who may have been emotionally unavailable or even mentally ill.

If you grew up with a mother at all, you expected to be taken care of physically, financially, emotionally and spiritually. That's what a mother is supposed to do. Unfortunately, when you don't get that, you don't stop longing for it; you miss what you didn't have.

You miss the compliments and the feelings of being loved.
You miss feeling valued and special.

Most importantly, you miss a crucial building block to your foundation of self-esteem and self-worth.

Your mother (the one who birthed you or chose you to adopt) is the one person in this world who can make you believe that you are important no matter what happens — good or bad. Therefore, our warped thinking becomes more like: "If my mother doesn't believe in me, then I must be worthless."

And that is simply not true.

In order to change what my Uncle Erik calls this "stinkin' thinkin'," we must first take a real honest look back at ourselves. I don't suggest going as far back as childhood because you really didn't know who you were and you were just beginning to learn right from wrong concretely. The exception to this would be if you clearly can remember some significant loss, abuse, neglect, or mistreatment that affected or changed you as a child (or that changed your mother). As teenagers and young adults, you began to understand the consequences of your actions. So, start there.

You knew that telling a lie would come back to bite you. You knew that unprotected sex could lead to pregnancy or disease. You knew not studying would lead to failure. You knew that whatever choices you made would come with consequences — good or bad. You began to establish your identity and decide who you wanted to be.

So, let's take a look back into your teenage and young adult years.

What did you like to do?

What did you believe about yourself?

What did you believe about the world?

Were you really as bad as your mother made you out to be?

Was the world really not open to your existence?

What goals did you have for yourself?
Did you believe that you could achieve the goals you set?
Or were you discouraged?

Did you have friends?

Did you laugh a lot? Did you smile?
Do you remember having fun?

Or were you depressed or afraid?

Did you feel that your mother didn't like you?

Did other adults seem to like you or think of you
differently than your mother?

I remember wanting to be a pediatrician; then
deciding I'd rather be a nurse. My mother always
said, "Why do you want to be a nurse? If you can
be a nurse, you should just go on to medical school
and be a doctor." What I know now is that, as a
nurse, I get to spend much more personal time with
my patients and really get to know them. I would
not get nearly that much time as a doctor, but I
would get more money. My mother was right about
that part.

So, I did initially go to college as a pre-med major;
but I envied my classmates who were pursuing
nursing. They seemed much more fulfilled than I.
When I failed organic chemistry, I gave up on
myself and decided I couldn't be a doctor anyway.
After so many emotional struggles, I realized a new
fascination with psychology; so I got a degree in
that.

I don't think my mom was ever happy with that

choice. I did go on to get an A in organic chemistry and a second degree in nursing, as well as, a graduate degree in psychology. At the writing of this book, I have completed my coursework and am writing my dissertation for a Doctorate in Psychology (PsyD) in Sport & Performance Psychology.

My mother insisted that I was "selfish" for pursuing a Master's degree because that "was time I could've been spending with my daughter." Now, I am a practicing RN and Licensed Professional Counselor (LPC); and am starting my new career as a sport psychologist. I love all my different careers, and still have great moments with my daughter.

Unfortunately, or maybe fortunately, I took the long route to fulfilling my destiny and finding joy in what I do for a living.

My mother and grandmother reluctantly came to my graduate school graduation. My aunt and uncle, that I mentioned in the beginning of the book, came down on the field to make sure I saw them cheering for me.

Go figure.

My mom gave some toast at my reception that I can't even remember because it felt so fake. Little did people know she had asked me to forego my graduation and reception so that I could attend the graduation of another family member who had taken eight years to finish a Bachelor's degree and had told the family she would not be marching — that is, until I announced I was graduating the same weekend.

Coincidence? Maybe.

Around Christmas, I had another family member graduate and a small reception was held for her by my mother's family. At that celebration, I mentioned that I had graduated from graduate school since no one in my family (on my mother's side) had even acknowledged my accomplishment. My grandmother responded with, "Well, maybe at some point, you will use one of these many degrees you have." Mind you, I went to graduate school while working as a full-time nurse and single mom.

At that moment, I saw my mother in her mother.

What if her mother had been wrong about her?

What if that same callous, negative attitude was what my mother grew up with all her life?

What if she had never been able to develop a sense of self?

What if she saw herself in me and was afraid that I would make some of the same mistakes she did?

Although it would not take away the hurt, that would shed some light on some things. That would explain a little bit of why my mother was the mother she was. All this time that I have been waiting for her to be someone different, have I missed an opportunity to be a blessing to my mother?

I wonder.

Sometimes it seems as though I held out for the fairy-tale ending and never got it.

To this day, my mom is not the first person I call about anything. In fact, there are many things that I censor or simply do not share with her because, at 44 years old, I still fear the berating and humiliation that still sometimes comes when we talk. As much as I wish my mother and I had the kind of relationship that you see on TV, or like Rashan and my Aunt Joyce, or like my friend, Lisa, and her mom, Connie, the reality is that we don't.

We never have.

When I finally realized that I wasn't going to get my emotional needs met through my mother, I was able to grieve my loss and move on.

> *"No one, however powerful and successful, functions well as an adult if his parents are not satisfied with him."*
> Frank Pittman III, M.D. (1935-2012); American psychiatrist and author

Contemplation: What do you need emotionally? Do you need someone to listen, to not judge, to be supportive? Do you need hugs, kisses, compliments, or gifts? Is there something you need your mother to do for you? Or do you just want to spend some mother-daughter time? Have you ever gotten what you need from your mother? Have you asked for it? Realistically, at this point in your life, do you think you will ever get it – the way you need it? If so, how can you make it happen? If not, can you let it go and find another way to meet your needs?

To feel loved and emotionally fulfilled, I need:

_____
_____
_____
_____
_____
_____
_____
_____
_____
_____
_____
_____
_____
_____

4 *GRIEF*

"There are no mistakes, no coincidences. All events are blessings given to us to learn from." Elisabeth Kübler-Ross

Grief. That's what this process is. In her 1969 book, *On Death and Dying*, Elisabeth Kübler-Ross identified five stages of grief — *denial*, *anger*, *bargaining*, *depression*, and *acceptance*. Kübler-Ross applied these stages to any form of catastrophic, personal loss. However, she also made it clear that the stages do not necessarily go in order — nor does every person experience every stage. The most common thread in the Kübler-Ross model is an individual's inability to change the tragic situation.

If people could find a way out of the pain or a solution to the travesty, they could stop grieving and start healing. When you are a child or teenager dependent on your mother, there is seemingly no way out of the pain, and no solution to your travesty of a life, that is not drastic.

Believe me, I ran through every scenario I could think of to end my pain and suffering. I thought of going to live with my father. Unfortunately, he had a new family in which I felt I was not included.

I tried to run away and got caught. I was locked up in juvenile detention as an "incorrigible child" until I was "bailed out" by my father.

When my father returned me to my mother, because I was literally in fear of my life, I ran away again; this time to a halfway house. My father eventually found me there and took me to his house.

I stayed with my father less than a year. That was like jumping from the frying pan into the fire. My dad traveled almost weekly for his job. So, every time he left, my stepmother would use that opportunity to tell me how much my family (including my father) hated me. She would call me names and treat me like crap. Believe me, she was not shy, or afraid, about letting me know that I was not welcome in *their new family*. She and I are surprisingly somewhat close today; but, back then, she was hell on wheels!

I left my dad's and went back to my mother's to receive an exchange student we had coming for the school year. Ironically, she turned out to be more of a problem child than I was. Funny!

Eventually, my mother, brother, and I moved back

to Texas where my mom's family was. Changing my residence did not, however, end my pain.

I tried twice to commit suicide in high school and survived.

I tried again in college, was hospitalized, and was kept from speaking to my parents because the hospital staff recognized how much they antagonized me.

I tried again as an adult and got no response from my mother that I can remember. My father was the first person I saw when I finally woke up and realized that I was handcuffed to a hospital bed. He looked at me and said, "You were really serious this time, huh? You really wanted outta here." I believe in that moment, I felt the deepest sadness ever. Not only had God saved me, but my father was again mocking my pain.

I knew then, that there was no way out of the hell on Earth that I called my life.
Please do not think that I take any of my attempts lightly or that I had no emotions when it was happening. Being suicidal is one of the most scary, empty, lonely places to be emotionally. In the actual moments that I attempted, there were a lot of tears, a deep, seemingly unending loneliness, fear, and even excruciating physical pain. Immediately afterward, there was a sense of relief, honestly. Upon awaking, there was more anger than sadness. And eventually, there was a sense of nothingness.

After you have hurt for so long, you just become numb. And sometimes, numb feels good simply because of the absence of hurt.

Looking back, I shake my head and feel pity for myself that I had to endure that kind of pain and sadness. However, I am proud of myself for making it through. I can recount those dark experiences, of truly wishing to be dead, in this book only because of all the therapy I have had and the work I have done to heal.

I understand the seriousness of what I attempted to do. I understand that I was really minutes from death. I understand that suicide is an option for more people than may admit it. And I want you to know that although there are still times that the *thought* pops in my head, suicide is no longer an option for me and will never be again. I hope you can find the power to make another choice as well.

I believe my teenage years were spent in the "denial" phase of the Kübler-Ross model.

I definitely did not want to believe that my mother could be treating me the way she was and that our relationship was incredibly terrible because of me. I could not understand how my friends seemed to have such good relationships with their mothers.

End of high school, through college, and early adulthood is where the "anger" began. I am not sure with whom I was angry, though. Was it my mom or myself? I know I was angry that I had very few, if any, good memories. I was angry that I didn't have a confidant in my mother like other women did. I was angry that I never had the fairy-tale.

The only "bargaining" I can remember is when I would try to bargain with God and beg Him to please stop the pain or just let me die. The bargaining was enmeshed, I believe, with the depression.

The depression I felt was overwhelming. There are no words, still today, to describe that kind of emptiness. Feeling so worthless and feeling so much pain that you absolutely, without fear, welcome death. That is a frighteningly dark place that I never want to revisit.

But, I am still here today, you say.

Yes, because, thank God, none of my suicide attempts were successful. The last time, I was very close, but no cigar. God had other plans for me.

That is not to say that I woke up from that last deep sleep, saw the light, saw God and found His peace.

That just means that I was not dead.

Reason for being
I began to realize that God had a purpose for me on this planet, if I didn't have one for myself. God had

a purpose for me, even if my mother saw none for me. I began to seek help outside of a liquor bottle or wine bottle and really started dealing with my psychological demons.

I had a psychiatric nurse, during my 30-day vacation in Charter Hospital in Atlanta whose name I cannot remember to this day; but I remember her face clearly. She was East Indian, slightly rotund, and had long, jet black hair that she kept pulled back in a braid. That woman held me in her lap one night, when all the other patients were sleeping, and let me cry for 45 minutes straight. And all she said the whole time was, "It's okay, Baby. Just let it out. Just let it out." She stroked my hair and rocked back and forth like she was my mother. I was 23 years old.

That was the first time I had ever felt comfort like that. That was the first time no one was afraid or dismissive of my pain. That was the first time I had ever let anyone know how deep my pain went. That was the first time I ever felt valued — like my feelings mattered.

I thought I would never stop crying that night. Thank you, God, for that angel. Thank You, for the grace, mercy, love, and compassion that You allowed to flow through her and to wash me. If I could find her, I would hug her tight and never want to let go. Wherever she is, Lord, let her know that she saved a life that night.

After that day, I began to face my sadness head on and I was doing it sober for the first time in a long time. I had learned very early how to self-medicate. Now, I chose to forge ahead with just me and God.

I floated in and out of depression for years. I would get a little stronger, crumple a little, then get back up and keep moving forward. I had good counselors throughout my journey. I had a graduate program that made me deal with some issues as well.

I began to understand who I was as a person. I began to figure out some of the things I wanted to accomplish in my life. I began to seek out my purpose in life. My mother had been wrong about me. I was strong, bright, and capable. I was not a quitter. I was not used, dirty linen. I was a child of The King and I had a purpose in this life.

The first "purpose" I came upon was being a mother. I was engaged to my daughter's father, but was not planning to be a mother first. However, when you choose to be disobedient to the word of God, and fornicate, things can happen.

My daughter was not an accident
One out of 200 women goes into menopause in their early twenties. I was the lucky one out of 200. The only way to "reverse" this phenomenon, according to my gynecologist, was to have a baby and sort of "reboot" my system into understanding that I was only 24 years old. Since I was engaged to be

married, my fiancé and I decided to try to get pregnant. We tried for a year with no success; so, I gave up and prayed that God's will be done. I was actually scheduled for a hysterectomy when I found out I was pregnant.

So, now, surely you think, my mom and I became close with the birth of my daughter. Nope. In fact, when I reluctantly told her I was pregnant, my mom spent 56 minutes on the phone, yelling at the top of her lungs: "March down to the clinic right now and get an abortion!"

I only found out later "through the grapevine" that my mom had an abortion before conceiving me. So, she knew all about it.

It saddens me that she couldn't just tell me, "Renee, I've been where you are. This is not a good decision right now and I think you should have an abortion."

I wish she would have talked to me about being a single parent.

I wish she would have talked to me about how hard it would be to go to school and work with a baby in tow.

Unfortunately, she did what she always did — yelled and made me feel like crap. That didn't help. So, instead of listening to any sound advice that was in the midst of her torrential spewing, I became defiant and had my daughter anyway. My mother never asked about my pregnancy. My father stopped speaking to me. Their shared opinion was, "That is a decision you made for your life and we do not have to be a part of it."

And they were absolutely right.

At age 26, I gave birth, eight weeks early, to a four pound, one ounce baby girl, who died during delivery. My daughter, Zari Sahar, had to be resuscitated right in front of my eyes. I knew then that God had a purpose for her as well and had entrusted me with her heart, her mind, and her soul.

Only after Zari's birth did my parents get involved in that part of my life. My father was glued to the NICU window after Zari was born, professing her beauty. My mother bought cases of preemie diapers and showed me how to burp my four-pound little girl without feeling like I was going to crush her.

My hope, of course, was to show Zari everything my mother never showed me. It was rough. I made it through nursing school with Honors; and I have set an example for my daughter, in the process, about never giving up in the face of adversity.

Although I did not want her to take the path I have taken, I do not love her any less when she makes choices with which I do not agree.

I make sure that she understands that I will stand by

her even if my heart is breaking.

And I pray that my daughter will feel like she can come to me prior to making any major decision that she is unsure about. That way, I can guide her into the best decision for her — instead of ridiculing her for making the worst decision.

That is where a lot of my sadness lies. Knowing that when big things happen in my life, I can't call my mom about it for fear that she will steal my joy.

When I was getting married, it took a schedule adjustment for her to pencil in my wedding. When I mistakenly shared with her that my husband and I were thinking of having a child together, her response was, "Ugh! I hope the two of you won't do that!"

Wow!

I knew who I wouldn't be calling with the good news. I miss that. I can always call my aunt. I can even call my stepmother. Neither of them takes the place, however, of the person who is supposed to love me most on this Earth.

So, what do you do?

You begin to understand that it doesn't matter.

That's right.

You can lead a horse to water, but you can't make him drink.

I can beg, cry, and plead with my mother; but it is not going to make her be someone she is not or make her love me in a different way, even if that is what I need.

The only two times I can even remember my mother telling me she was proud of me were when I went to the Dominican Republic to do some missionary work in a clinic in 2000 and in my Mother's Day card in 2009.

In the Dominican Republic, when I heard the person on the other end of the phone say, "Well, I am very proud of you, Renee, for what you are doing over there," I almost dropped the phone. I thought the operator had connected me to the wrong number.

After not being on drugs or arrested, getting three degrees, receiving a commission in the Air Force, and raising a great daughter as a single mom, she was proud of me for going to the Dominican Republic to help the sick. Had I only known that is what it would take?

I cherish those two moments, however, because they're the only times I can remember "I'm proud of you" ever being said and I may not ever hear it again. So, I keep the memories tucked away in a special place.

That's who my mother is, though. I cannot change her core being.

Does she love me?
Absolutely, yes.

Does she like me?
According to her own words, no;
but the jury continues to deliberate on that one.

Is she proud of me?
I think so.

Is she my best friend?
No.

Would I share my deepest, darkest secret with her?
Absolutely not.

Do I think she could do better?
Maybe, but who am I to judge?

She is who she is.

And she is my mother.

"A daughter without her mother is a woman broken.
It is a loss that turns to arthritis and settles deep
into her bones." Kristin Hannah

Contemplation: What is the reality of your relationship with your mother? Not what it could be or what you want it to be – what is the *reality* of your relationship? Can you grieve the loss of your dream relationship? If you're already there, what stage of grief are you in? Are you moving through the grief process or are you stuck?

Write a "goodbye" letter to your dream mother-daughter relationship and let it rest in peace.

5 *ACCEPTANCE*

> *"Acceptance doesn't mean resignation;*
> *it means understanding that something is*
> *what it is and that there's got to be a way*
> *through it. "* Michael J. Fox

So, how do you finally get to acceptance?

You begin to realize that you have to accept people where they are in life.

You have to accept people for who they are.

You have to accept people where they are emotionally.

I had to understand that my mother had gone through her own struggles. My mother had suffered her own damage. And my mother was who she was and that was not going to change. Had she gone to therapy, maybe it would have; but she did not believe in that and that was her opinion.

But because of what she went through in her life, the emotional abuse that she suffered growing up, I think she had her own questions about who she was as a woman, who she was a mother. I think my father, no; I'm sure my father, made her question who she was as a wife.

Don't get me wrong. My mother is extremely successful and I am incredibly proud of her for continuing to climb the corporate ladder and not letting my father's leaving completely devastate her life.

My mother is the CEO and President of a major international airport. She is one of the few females in aviation. She is an attractive, intellectual, articulate, powerful, well-liked, respected leader in her field. Other people's experience of my mother, **however**, is very different than mine. Sometimes, I even have trouble wrapping my brain around the woman I see in a television news interview and the woman I saw raise me.

The beginning of acceptance
But, acceptance began to come when I realized that I had to learn to fulfill my own needs. When I learned that no matter what I needed from my

mother emotionally, she was not capable of giving it to me and there was nothing I could do to change that.

I felt for a long time that my mother did not like me as a person. I always knew on a spiritual level that my mother loved me because I was her daughter. But, I never truly believed that she liked me as a person and I couldn't figure out why. Granted, I had not been the easiest teenager to deal with, but I think I turned out okay as an adult.

I remember at my brother's college graduation reception, my mother made a toast and she said (about my brother), "Even if he wasn't my son, I would still want him as a part of my life because he is a wonderful person." After three graduations, I don't remember one toast that my mother gave that would have affected me like that. And I can only imagine what my brother felt knowing that even if he wasn't her son, she would still want him in her life.

Sadly, I never got the impression that my mother felt that way about me; and as much as I tried to explain that to my family, no one understood. The general consensus was: "That's impossible," "You're making that up," and "You have issues that you need to deal with if you feel that way."

Well, let me tell you, one Christmas, my mother let me have it! I've told you repeatedly throughout this book that my mother yells. My mother is a screamer. And to this day, I do not know what triggered this confrontation; but in front of my entire family and some holiday guests, my mother finally let the truth come out. She said to me, in my face, that she "could not stand me!" That she "could not understand why I was even on this Earth!"

She ranted and raved about how sorry she felt for my daughter that she had me for a mother. We were in Dallas, TX. My daughter was standing there. She was four and she was frightened. My family stood there, mouths open, in disbelief because everything I had said for years had just come true.

I picked up my daughter to leave. My brother asked me not to get on the road because it was a 12-hour drive back to Atlanta. But I had to go; because at that moment, I knew that I had to protect myself and I had to protect my daughter. I did not want this generational disease to spread any further.

I remember my mother screaming, "Get out! Go! Nobody wants you here anyway!" As much as one of my aunts tried to get her to calm down, even pulling her out of the room, my mother came back with even more venom.

And then my mother's mother said, "Why do you upset your mother so?" I had no words to even answer my grandmother because I had done nothing to provoke the vicious, verbal, and emotional attack that my mother had just given to me.

Yet, again, I was accused of being wrong and upsetting her.

On my drive home from Dallas that night, the adrenalin was flowing (thank God, because I had been up all day). The tears streamed down my face, probably until I got to Mississippi.

I guess as much as I felt that my mother did not like me, it was harder to actually hear it. To see the disgust on her face and the rage in her eyes and to not know what I had done, beyond simply existing, to evoke such hatred from the person who carried me and gave birth to me.

It's a moment of devastation that I cannot even put into words on paper. It is an image that is seared into my mind and my heart.

It is an image that I doubt I will ever forget.

Just like I won't forget when my mother almost choked me to death until my lips turned gray and my brother literally jumped on her back to get her to let go. I remember that same look. That day and Christmas day — that look of "I wish you were dead" or "I wish you weren't here."

Sometimes I wonder if my mother wished that one of my suicide attempts had been successful. I will never know because I will never ask her. I'm not sure that I could handle her response.

But, something snapped that Christmas night. A light bulb came on for me that my mother was clueless about who I was and that she had no desire to even find out. So, at that point, I stopped hoping for it. I stopped looking for her to make deposits in my love bank.

I accepted the fact that she was who she was; and as much or as little as she loved me, *she did not like me as a person* and that was going to have to be okay. I refused to take phone calls from my mother for about a year. I refused to take phone calls from anyone on that side of the family. I asked them to all lose my number because in the thick of that vicious confrontation, not one person defended me.

Not one person stood up for me.

Not one person protected me.

They tried to calm my mother down, but *nobody said to her, "You're wrong."* Nobody said to her, "You're wrong about Renee" or "You're wrong for the way you treat Renee."

Nobody said anything.

So, I asked them not to call me — not to have any contact with me — because I needed to heal and strengthen myself so that I could handle the vicious negativity and pessimism that comes from that side of the family. I was not rude about it. I simply asked them not to call. The couple of times they did try to call, I just wouldn't answer the phone.

I continued to let my mother speak to her granddaughter because what was going on between my mother and I had nothing to do with their relationship. My daughter, being a child, would always say, "Mommy, do you want to talk to Mimi?" And I would simply answer, "No."

My acceptance was the end of my grieving and I had to finish grieving so that I could let go. I had to realize that I was okay just being me.

I am okay simply existing.

I had permission and purpose from God Almighty to be a member of this society.

I did tell my mother, that Christmas night, it would be the very last time that she would disrespect me and the very last time that she would ever hurt me. I told her that I did not appreciate her actions in front of my daughter. I let her know that I was finally going to stand up for myself. I was finally going to stop looking to her to make me feel whole.

Again, I sought therapy.

Again I got into the Word.

I had some family members try to tell me that my

mother was jealous of me and that's why she was never happy for me. I don't believe that. I cannot wrap my brain around the concept of a mother being jealous of a child. When I look at my daughter, I want more for her than I had for myself and there is no jealousy in that. So, I don't buy the whole jealousy theory.

My mother is who she is and that is really all I can say. I do not know her entire history. I do know some of the good and some of the bad. But, I don't know how my mother dealt with any of it. I don't expect her to go any farther than she does. I don't expect her to be lovey-dovey, touchy-feely, or overly affectionate with me. I don't even expect my mother to like me because I know she doesn't.

Here's the kicker: I DON'T CARE. I have finally reached a point in my life where it doesn't matter. I don't even think about what my mother would think of me or how my mother would feel. I know whatever her thoughts and feelings are, they will be negative.

So, I don't even let it cross my mind. That may be sad to some people; but to me, that is victory. That is acceptance because there is no more hurt, pain, or sadness associated with it. It is just a simple fact that I can state without any emotion. My mother's feelings about me, toward me, are her own. I don't ask her about them because I don't care to know.

I simply continue to live my life and do what I do

and be the best person that I think I can be. My mother's approval or disapproval is almost never a factor in the decisions that I make.

I guess it was a factor when it came to publishing this book, though. I was very concerned that my mother's disapproval would be finite and concrete once the book was published. As much as I had reconciled my own reality of my relationship with my mother, a microscopic particle of hope probably remained hidden deep in my spirit. Publishing this book could mean the loss of even that microscopic particle. Oh, well.

My mother and I do talk occasionally. It is definitely not one of those Hallmark moments. It is more of a "checking in" to make sure that she's okay. She'll check on me to make sure I'm okay. We talk about extended family concerns. We talk about what's going on in her life and my brother's life. Never is the discussion about what's going in my life because I choose not to share. We never discuss feelings about anything and that's by choice. Conversations are typically over the phone or via text or email. If we are ever face-to-face, I always stand a little to my left so that I can visualize her words passing by my right ear instead of going directly into my heart. That is how I protect myself and maintain my sanity.

I accept my mother today for who she is with all her emotional limitations. I enjoy watching her relationship with her granddaughter. I am happy that they are able to make happy memories together because I don't have that many with my mother. In fact, I have very few. So, I am glad to know that my daughter, at least, can have some.

And that's good.

So, how do you get to acceptance?

Acceptance comes with compassion. Acceptance may or may not come with understanding, but it does come with compassion. Acceptance comes by understanding that your mother is who she is. Her personality and her inner core developed based on her abundance or lack of whatever.

But, without intense therapy or divine intervention, she is not going to change. That does not make her right. She can still be wrong about you, about life, about your children, about your spouse (or significant other). *She can still be wrong.*

But, acceptance comes when you realize that her views come from whatever *tint is on her glasses* that causes her warped outlook.

Acceptance comes when you understand that *your mother is not capable*, without help, of meeting your needs the way you need them to be met.

Acceptance comes when there is *no volatile emotion* affiliated with that revelation.

Acceptance comes when you are able to *fill your own emotional tank.*

> *"Love yourself first and everything else falls into line. You really have to love yourself to get anything done in this world."* Lucille Ball

Contemplation: Have you gotten to acceptance? How do you feel about your mother and your relationship with your mother – right now, in this moment? If you are not at acceptance yet, can you see yourself working towards it? It's not easy. It comes with tears, anger, sadness, and sometimes, even relief. Again, look at the *reality* of your relationship with your mother – remembering from where your mother came, how she was raised, and how she learned to love – then, find compassion for her and forgive her.

Write a letter of forgiveness to your mother (for your sake). You don't have to give it to her. Perhaps, acceptance will come, for you, then.

6 *LIKE MOTHER, LIKE DAUGHTER?*

"A mother who radiates self-love and self-acceptance actually vaccinates her daughter against low self-esteem." Author Unknown

So, what have I been wrong about when it comes to my daughter?

Have I written only good things on her soul over the last 18 years?

Absolutely not. I have made some mistakes. I have said some hurtful things. I have made her cry and that hurts me deeply.

My daughter has reminded me of a "look" that I have that frightens her. It's a look that — she feels — might mean that I don't love her.

I hate that look. I hate that anything I might do or say would wound my beautiful daughter and scar her innocence. I don't think that I have said anything to her that will affect her until she is my age. At least, I pray that I haven't. Zari always has the opportunity to tell me, however, if I have done or said something that is hurtful.

My report card
As I mentioned earlier (in the Acknowledgements), when my daughter would get her report card, I would get my report card from her as well. My first report card was painful.

At first, my articulate, outspoken daughter would not look at me or open her mouth. She was about seven or eight years old. We were in the car and I was explaining to her that I wanted her to be totally honest with me about what I was doing right and what I was doing wrong as a parent. I promised her that there would be no repercussions — only change.

I don't think she believed me initially. We drove a little while longer and I begged her to tell me how I could improve.

Finally, she spoke. She said, "You're a good mom." I encouraged her to continue because I knew there was a "but" coming. She continued, "I mean...I know I need discipline; but do you think you could praise me a little more? Sometimes you yell at me about what I'm doing wrong more than you tell me that you are proud of me."

Whoa! What a blow to my ego! Here I was thinking that I was doing everything right so that my daughter would not feel like I felt as a child. Yet, with her own truth, she had let me know that I was missing the mark. She noticed that there was more focus on the negative than the positive and that mattered to her.

Thank goodness I asked. I probably would not have figured it out until she was an adult and said something to me like, "Mom, I never felt like you were proud of me" or "Mom, I never felt like I was ever good enough."

I was beginning to repeat the same cycle I had fought so hard to stop.

So, I had one semester to change my behavior. I began to make a conscious effort to notice what she did that was good — grades, behaviors, tasks, etc. — and I made sure to let her know how proud I was of her. I continued to discipline; but I made sure to mix some "warm fuzzies" in with the "cold pricklies." In fact, I tried to make sure that the "warm fuzzies" outweighed the "cold pricklies" in both quantity and quality.

It was not easy. Negativity was ingrained in who I was as a person and a mother. It was the way I had been parented and it was all that I knew. I would bring home a grade of 98 and instead of, "Great job!" I got, "What happened to the other two points?"

Changing my parenting style was hard, but I convinced myself that I could always do better.

When the next semester came, I braced myself. I wasn't sure if I had done enough to change the way my daughter saw me. I wasn't sure that she even noticed a change.

So, it was time. I asked my daughter, "Has Mommy done any better?"

She answered, with a huge smile, "Yes, Mommy, you have been doing much better! Thank you!" Then, without me prompting her, she said, "Now, what you need to work on is spending more time with me. I want to do some things together, just you and me."

So, I had improved my "communication" score from a <u>D</u> to maybe a <u>B</u>. Now, unfortunately, I was failing in "quality time." I was happy and dismayed at the same time. The good thing, though, was that my efforts had been noticed and I was being given another chance to correct some more of my work.

So, I took the challenge and began to plan some mommy-daughter days — manicures, pedicures, hair, pictures, shopping — whatever came to mind. She and I really enjoyed those days. I don't think my daughter realizes how much they meant to me. They were a struggle to plan with all the work I have to do; but they were well worth it.

In the mommy-daughter days I got to see who my daughter really was, beyond who I thought she was or wanted her to be.

I cherish her beautiful smile and her hearty laughter. I cherish all the memories we make. I cherish the opportunity to get to watch her change and grow from day to day. I get to see her silly side, her serious side, her spiritual side, her friendly side, her selfish side, her vulnerable side, her compassionate side, her inquisitive side, and her intellectual side.

I get to see HER – as a person I want in my life – not just because she's my daughter!

The more time we spent together, the closer we got. We would communicate about our mother-daughter relationship constantly. Those conversations could be difficult; but they were always productive.

My heart broke about two years after my first report card when I read a poem my daughter wrote about how unhappy she was and how things might be better if she was not here. When we sat down to talk, I immediately heard myself 20 years ago. My daughter said to me, "I just don't feel that you like me, Mommy. I know you love me; but I don't think you like me and sometimes, I even think you hate me."

Here I was thinking that I was doing pretty good at

parenting. I had made all the changes that my daughter had wanted and needed. What I hadn't done is remain consistent. I had once again let life overwhelm me and the stress was oozing out even when I thought it wasn't.

My daughter was getting a vibe from me that overshadowed my actions and my positive words. She saw pain in my face and heard stress in my voice. And as children do, she internalized that and assumed it was her fault.

I again had to reassure her that none of my adult issues were because of her and I had to show her that I meant what I said. I had to learn to put my concerns and my frustrations about work, money, relationships, etc. away when I was with Zari and focus on her and all the good feelings she brought.

I had to dig deeper to meet her needs and speak her love language.

I had to remind myself who my daughter was and how special her mere existence was to me.

That is the most awesome moment in the life of a parent — at least it was for me. That moment when you realize that you don't just love your child because he or she is your child; but you actually like them for the little person that they are with their own thoughts, dreams, and personality. It changes how you see your child forever.

And when you thought you could not love them more than you already did, it sends your love to a new depth in your soul.

So, I guess I understand where my mother was coming from when she said that "even if my brother wasn't her son, she would still want him in her life because he is a great person." She had that defining moment at some time with my brother — she had come to like him for the person he was and her love for him was, and still is, very deep.

As I write this book, I am actually happy for my mother - that she had that moment with at least one of her children. I know how that feels with my own daughter. Of course, I still wish that my mother could have had that moment with me. But, again, that is not my reality.

I wish my efforts had paid off with my own daughter; and that she was happy and successful because of all the love I thought I poured into her. But, that is not my reality either. My daughter has chosen a different path for herself – a hard one – and that hurts like hell.

The difference is, I don't feel like I failed my daughter, emotionally, the way my mother failed me; and my daughter agrees. She tells me all the time that I am a good mother, that she loves me, and that she knows I love her. She has simply decided that she wants to follow her own path in life no matter where it takes her.

I wish the heavens would open up and a single sunray would shine down on me so that my mother might see me in a different light and love me unconditionally – the way I love Zari.

Healing the little girl inside
That's the little girl in me who still longs for all she missed. As I interact with my own daughter, in a way, I try to heal the little girl in me too.

I try to assure my inner child that little girls don't always get hurt by their mothers.

I try to let her see that her suffering has saved another little girl (Zari) from the same pain.

Emotionally, I thank my inner child for being so brave all those years and for looking out for my daughter — for reminding me of the pain I could cause and the damage I could do.

To the little girl in me, I say:

> *It's okay now. We made it through and you can rest now. You don't have to protect me anymore and you don't have to protect Zari from me. I will take care of you and Zari so that neither of you will ever question your self-worth or my love for you. I*

understand the longing you have that things had been different. Unfortunately, things may never be different; so, you can grow up now knowing that I truly love you, I appreciate you tremendously, and I am incredibly proud of you.

> *"She held herself until the sobs of the child inside subsided entirely. I love you, she told herself. It will all be okay."* H. Raven Rose, *Shadow Selves*

Contemplation: For those of you who have children, it's time to get a report card. Grade yourself first; then, ask your children to grade you. You can use the report cards Zari and I developed, which I have provided for you, or you can create your own.

PARENTAL REPORT CARD – SELF-EVALUATION					
Criteria	**1ST Qtr**	**2nd Qtr**	**3rd Qtr**	**4th Qtr**	**Final**	**Comments**
Affection & Love • Give hugs & kisses • Tell them "I love you" • Make them feel loved						
Praise & Discipline • Balanced equally • Appropriate rewards & punishments • Rules/expectations are clear • Rules/expectations are reasonable • Fair & consistent						
Respect • Their privacy & things • Their thoughts & feelings • Don't curse them or call them names • Set a good example for them						

Understanding & Support • Understand their feelings • Understand life from their perspective • Not quick to judge them • Help with homework/ problems • Attend their events					
Freedom & Responsibility • Allow them to have friends over or go out with friends • Give them a chance to do what I asked or meet expectations					
Quality Time • We do fun things together • Enjoy spending time with them					
Communication • Patiently listen to them • Don't talk over them • Ask about their day & their interests					

Knowledge • Really know THEM or at least show genuine interest in knowing them					
Safety & Security • Provide food & shelter • Don't keep secrets from them • They can trust what I say • I keep my word					
Smiles & Mood • Smile at them • Direct moods appropriately					

PARENTAL REPORT CARD – CHILD/TEEN EVALUATION						
Criteria	1ST Qtr	2nd Qtr	3rd Qtr	4th Qtr	Final	Com-ments
Affection & Love • Gives hugs & kisses • Tells me "I love you" • Makes me feel loved						
Praise & Discipline • Balanced equally • Appropriate rewards & punishments • Rules/expectations are clear • Rules/expectations are reasonable • Fair & consistent						
Respect • My privacy & my things • My thoughts & feelings • Doesn't curse me or call me names • Sets a good example for me						

Understanding & Support • Understands my feelings • Understands life from my perspective • Is not quick to judge me • Helps with homework/ problems • Attends my events					
Freedom & Responsibility • Allows me to have friends over or go out with friends • Gives me a chance to do what I've been asked to do or to meet expectations					
Quality Time • We do fun things together • Enjoys spending time with me					
Communication • Patiently listens to me • Doesn't talk over me • Asks about my day & my interests					

Knowledge • Really knows ME or at least shows a genuine interest in knowing me					
Safety & Security • Provides food & shelter • Doesn't keep secrets from me • I can trust what they say • They keep their word					
Smiles & Mood • Smiles at me • Directs moods appropriately					

7 *MORE THAN JUST A TEACHER*

"One looks back with appreciation to the brilliant teachers, but with gratitude to those who touched our human feelings. The curriculum is so much necessary raw material, but warmth is the vital element for the growing plant and for the soul of the child."

Carl Gustav Jung (1875-1961) -
Swiss psychologist and psychiatrist

One day in the spring of 1988, a teacher changed my life. My teenage years started with my parents' divorce and went downhill from there. I moved back to Texas from Georgia with my mother, with whom — you know by now — I had a very bad relationship. We never got along and I never felt that she cared.

In fact, after my parents divorced, I didn't feel that anyone loved me or cared about what happened to me.

My four-year battle with depression, my self-loathing, and my lack of hope all came to a head one night during my senior year at JJ Pearce High School. I remember crying while I wrote a goodbye letter to my family. I remember the sparkling silver of the razor blade and the thin, sharp blade. I remember cutting my wrists and I remember bleeding. Most of all, however, I remember that joyous feeling of relief that all my pain was finally over.

Then, morning came and I woke up. I was so angry with God that day that I was numb! I felt nothing on the inside — not joy, not sorrow, not pain, not hope — absolutely nothing but a cavernous emptiness. I was in a black hole, a vortex, from which I saw no way out. I was dead on the inside and figured no one would care. It surely did not matter to me.

I was a walking zombie.

When I got to school that day, my psychology teacher walked by me and said, "How are you doing today?"

I responded, "Not so good, Mr. Nelson. I tried to kill myself last night."

Most of us know that the typical person asks "How are you?" as a reflexive courtesy — automatically following "Hello" — not because they are truly interested in what's actually going on in someone's life. People walk by expecting to hear, "Fine" or "Good"; so they can keep walking with a clear conscience.

Thank God, Mr. Nelson was never "typical." That day, he became more than just a teacher. He became a ray of hope — a person who actually cared that I existed in the world. He cared that I was hurting.

Mr. Nelson took me to his room that morning and talked to me about what was going on in my life. He wanted to know from where my pain was coming and why it was consuming me to the point of wanting to die. Not once did he judge me or try to convince me that my feelings were wrong. In fact, all he said was, "I'm sorry." Then, the bell rang.

As I got up to leave, Mr. Nelson said, "I don't think you should be alone right now. Would you mind if I walked you to your class?" I said, "Sure," and assumed the rest of the day would pass by as usual. Surprisingly, Mr. Nelson was at the door when I came out of my 1st period class. He simply said, "I thought maybe I could walk you to your next class and see how you're doing." I had no words, but as much of a smile as I could muster. Mr. Nelson was at the door at the end of every class I had that day.

He seemed to really want to know that I was still alive and still making it through my day.

After school, Mr. Nelson walked me to the office where my mother was waiting. I am not sure if he called her or if someone else did; but she was there and she was pissed! Upon seeing her and the anger in her face, I went a million miles away in my head. I do not remember anything that was discussed between my mother, Mr. Nelson, the principal, and the counselor.

I really wasn't there. The pain my mother could cause me was suffocating and terrifying. I assumed that by the time we left that afternoon, everyone would know how worthless I was — even Mr. Nelson. My mom confirmed my minute value the minute we go into the car. She angrily told me, "If you ever have me called off my job, again, for something like this….wasting my time!" I actually laughed inside as I thought to myself, "Do you really think that I would call you for anything that would require you to care?" What a joke?!

This was the same woman I was trying to be away from forever. Yet, my suicide attempt was not worth her being called off her job.

We went directly from school to see our pastor. He was told that I had tried to commit suicide as though it was an annoyance more than a concern. My pastor told me that I would go to Hell if I killed myself — as though I cared. One thing I did not think about when I was committing suicide was Heaven versus Hell. I just wanted to be gone from *Earth*. I could care less where I ended up as long as I was not in my life.

I admit I got scared, though, when I heard myself say to my pastor, "It doesn't matter. There is no God anyway."

I knew in that moment that I had nothing left — not even my belief in God and He was my very last hope. I saw a counselor in the next day or two and my Dad flew through Dallas as well. He had a one or two hour layover; so, my Mom took me to the airport to talk to him.

Now, mind you, my father is no slacker. And I love him very much. Like, my mother, he is very successful. He is a well-respected, highly adored corporate attorney, in a major metropolitan city, who has only lost one case in the 30+ years that he's been practicing. He is handsome, articulate, powerful, patient, funny, and about as smart as Einstein, in my humble opinion. I mean, the man studied all of FOUR hours for the bar exam (the night before) and passed on his first attempt – impressive, I know. That same man, that everyone sees as wonderfully fantastic, could be as cold as ice.

So, at the airport, the conversation with my father went like this:

Dad: So, your mom tells me you tried to kill
     yourself.

Me: Yes, Sir.

Dad: What did you do?

Me: I cut my wrists.

Dad: Let me see.

(I turned my wrists over)

Dad: Hmm. You didn't cut too deep.

Me: No, Sir. Not deep enough.

Dad: Next time, use a gun and just shoot
     yourself. It's quicker.

Me: Okay. I'll do that.

Then, he patted me on the shoulder, waved at my
mother, turned around and got back on his plane,
flew to wherever he was going, and the subject was
not brought up again.

That was it. Mr. Nelson spent an entire school day
making sure that I was taken care of while my mom
spent all of two 30 minute car rides and my dad
spent about 20 minutes of a one-hour layover.

Honestly, though, I was glad all the hoopla was over. With no one paying attention, I could plan my next attempt and make sure that I did not fail. All I needed was to be left alone. Fortunately, Mr. Nelson continued to do everything in his power to make sure that I was not alone and I did not have the opportunity to plan another attempt.

He found me the first day I came back to school and asked me how things had gone after I left school with my mom. I told him about all of the "love and concern" I had received [from my Pastor]; and I saw my pain in his eyes. I'm sure he realized that I had not mentioned my parents. I was hoping he wouldn't cry because I had run out of tears.

Thankfully, he didn't, but he did ask me to promise that I would come by his room and check in with him from time to time throughout the day. I agreed. I liked Mr. Nelson. He always had a smile on his face and he always seemed to be enjoying life.

He made me wonder if maybe there was a reason to stick around in this life.

For the next three months or so, I dropped by Mr. Nelson's room throughout the school day and just stuck my head in so he could see me. Mr. Nelson's room was a safe place. There was a graffiti board in the back of the room where we could express our thoughts and feelings. More importantly, though, Mr. Nelson would always sit down when he talked to you – to let you know he was interested in what you had to say. I could honestly say that I first learned the art of paraphrasing from Bob Nelson because he did it so well. He was the only teacher I have ever known that always seemed to have time to talk to you or at least to listen.

Slowly, I began to smile again. Then, as graduation approached, I began to realize what Mr. Nelson had been trying to teach us in class every day. He had been teaching much more than Psychology 101 – more like Life 101.

He opened and ended every semester the same way — "I'm Bob Nelson. But my friends call me Mister." During the semester, he would use the phrase, "**Here I am**…taking roll…starting my lecture…passing out the test."

It was always funny; but I never really knew why he did that.

Then, I finally realized that what he was really saying was, "I'm me and I'm here; and for today, just existing as me is good enough." He didn't have to put on airs. He didn't have to be brilliant (even though I always thought he was). He didn't have to worry about yesterday or tomorrow. He was simply okay being Bob Nelson — simply existing in the world and being present each day. He mattered in the world and he made the best of every day he spent on the planet.

He mattered to me; and because of Bob Nelson, I finally mattered to myself.

Thank you, Dr. Nelson (he's Dr. Nelson now, but was Mr. Nelson in high school), for being more than just a teacher, but an inspiration — and thank you for challenging me to embrace the essence of this poem:

My Declaration of Self-Esteem

I AM ME

In all the world, there is no one else exactly like me. Everything that comes out of me is authentically me because I alone chose it. I own everything about me — my body, my feelings, my mouth, my voice, all my actions, whether they be to others or to myself. I own my fantasies, my dreams, my hopes, my fears. I own all my triumphs and successes, all my failures and mistakes because I own all of me. I can become intimately acquainted with me — by so doing, I can love me and be friendly with me in all my parts. I know there are aspects about myself that puzzle me, and other aspects that I do not know — but as long as I am friendly and loving to myself, I can courageously and hopefully look for solutions to the puzzles and for ways to find out more about me. However I look and sound, whatever I say and do, and whatever I think and feel at a given moment in time is authentically Me. If later some parts of how I looked, sounded, thought, and felt turn out to be unfitting, I can discard that which is unfitting, keep the rest, and invent something new for that which I discarded. I can see, hear, feel, think, say, and do. I have the tools to survive, to be close to others, to be productive, to make sense and order out of the world of people and things outside of me.

I own me; and therefore, I can engineer me.

I am me and   I AM OKAY.

Contemplation: Who was your Dr. Nelson? What did he or she teach you about yourself? What did he or she teach you about life? If you had a Dr. Nelson, then you can no longer say that "no one cared." So, embrace that reality – that at some point in your life, you mattered for some reason to someone.

Write a thank you note to your Dr. Nelson. Now, you have to figure out why you matter to yourself.

8 *LOOK IN THE MIRROR*

*"When a woman becomes her own best
friend life is easier."*
Diane Von Furstenberg

Usually when graffiti is spray painted on a wall, the city government will pay for it to be cleaned up. It gets washed away and is eventually forgotten. If the graffiti was politically charged, it might make the evening news, but eventually it is erased from our memories forever.

Soul graffiti, however, seems to never be forgotten. We can write things next to it. We can cross it out, but we still know that it is there. And at the most unexpected times, it rears its ugly head and reminds us that the words are still there. A trigger will be pushed for us and the silent whispers that linger become loud again, shouting, "You are a failure!"

"You are worthless!" "You are fat!" "No one loves you!" All of a sudden, we are right back in that awful place where we felt unworthy and "less than."

Does that mean that we will never get over the damage done by the words that were written on our souls?

Absolutely not!!!

However — and this is critical — we cannot wash away the graffiti if we don't look at it.

So, what was written on your soul as a child or young adult? This might be painful; but something about your graffiti and/or your longing to erase it, drew you to buy this book. The subtitle of this book, "What if your mother was wrong" may have sparked some hope; or, at least, raised the question, "What if she was wrong? Then, what does that mean for me?"

What did your mother (or father) say to you, or about you, that scarred your soul? What did he or she say that has stuck with you like a toxic, bloodstain — always lingering, no matter how many times you try to wash it away?

Were you told that you were ugly?

That you would never amount to anything?

Were you told that you were unwanted, unplanned,

a mistake?

Were you told that you were too dark or too pale?

Were you called stupid, worthless, ignorant, retarded?

Were you told that you were selfish?

Were you called fat or lazy?

Were you told, like me, that no one would ever want you — implying that you were forever unlovable?

Were you made to feel that, no matter what you did or said, you would never be good enough?

Were you told more than one of these things?

Were they said repeatedly?

Did those words, written on your soul, become your truth?

Has that soul graffiti hidden or tainted your true self?

When you look in the mirror, does it feel incongruent?

Do you get the sense, or want to believe, that those words do not define who you are?

Have you started to wonder if they ever really did?

New decisions

If you have decided, somewhere in your soul, that there are better words to describe you; then, good for you.

If you have decided that those words will no longer control your destiny; then, bravo.

If you have decided that the man or woman you have become is the antithesis of that graffiti-painted wall of shame; then I challenge you to take your power back.

I encourage you to change the tape that's playing in your head. Only **you** have the power to change the tape. ***Only you really know you well enough to define yourself truly.***

Look in the mirror.

Take a good long look. How do you look?

Not how your mother says you look. Not how other people say you look. How do you look to you?

*By your definition, **and your definition only**, how do you look?*

Don't be afraid to answer honestly. What do you like about you?

What would you like to change?

Why do you want to change it?

Are the changes you seek, realistic?

Would the physical changes alter who you are on the inside?

Contemplation: Now, pull out your list again – the list you were supposed to create back in the Soul Graffiti chapter. Let's revisit that. Look at the words by which you put a question mark. Are they true or not? Do you think they were said to you because of your mother's truth or experience? Do you think that they were said because your mother really didn't know you? Make a decision for yourself – right now – true or false – either cross the word out or put a checkmark by it. Now, look at the words you crossed out. Remind yourself that they are not true; then, ERASE them from the list, but more importantly, from your soul.

9 *GOOD ENOUGH*

*"What I am is good enough if I
would only be it openly."*
Carl Rogers

When you say, "I'll never be enough" — you are
absolutely right!

To those who *do not know you* and *don't want to
take the time* to get to know you, you may never be
enough.

To those who *wrote all the crap on your soul*, you
may never be enough.

To those who actually *think they know you*, but are
really clueless, you may never be enough.

To those who *don't really love you*, you may never
be enough.

To those who *do not have your best interest at heart*, you may never be enough.

So, yes, say it over and over again, a thousand times. "I may never be enough to those who do not know the real me, who do not love the real me, or do not have my best interest at heart."

"But, I will *always be good enough* for me."

That is the point to which we all must get.

We must get to a point where only what we think about ourselves matters.

We must get to a point where outside opinions, whether from family, friends, colleagues, or acquaintances, do not affect how we define ourselves.

Be prepared; it is not an easy endpoint. It is more of a *pinnacle* — but it can be reached. To get there, you must be willing to take an honest assessment of your whole self; and that can be painful. In order to heal a lifetime of pain, however, we must identify the source and the mechanism of injury. If you look at the journey in its entirety, it may seem too overwhelming.

So, let's take it in steps.

My inner child

Before we begin, allow me to introduce you to my inner child. We all have an inner child; he or she is not a splinter personality or anything like that. One's inner child is simply that part of us who helped us survive some difficult times growing up. It is on the soul of our inner child that the graffiti was originally written. He or she is not malicious; but rather has tried to protect your heart and spirit for many years. Unfortunately, when we reach adulthood, we must put away our childish ways.

So, meet my inner child:

> I am Renee's inner child. You can call me Mickey. I try to keep Renee from getting too upset about the graffiti written on her soul. There are words there like worthless, unlovable, failure, unattractive, and selfish. They don't really describe her, but she feels like they do. She hears the "tape" of her parents' voices endlessly looping.
>
> So, I tell her that we might as well just accept what they've said as who we are. It's not like her feelings have ever been, or will ever be, valued. I keep Renee very quiet about her feelings and I don't allow her to call a lot of people "friend." I keep her somewhat isolated and help her

maintain her independence. I kind of sit on the sidelines and wait for people to ask me to play while simultaneously dreading the invitation.

I realize that keeps Renee lonely sometimes; but it's better than having to open up to people and letting them get to know us. I'm always afraid that I am going to suck at what I'm asked to do and then, nobody will like me. I mean, if my parents don't like me, why would anyone else? My own mother told me she hated me once and she never took it back or apologized for saying it. So, it must be true, right?

I've tried really hard, but it seems like my efforts are never enough. I made good grades as a kid and believe I'm very smart; but unless I'm perfect, no one even seems to notice. In a way, it challenged me; and in a way, it exhausted me.

I never let Renee stop trying, though, because I still have a tiny bit of hope that one day, her parents will see all the good she has done. So, she can't start slacking now.

My dad left me for a different family. I don't know why I couldn't make him love me enough. When I tried to talk about my feelings about my stepmother or something, my dad would shut me down and then punish me later by excluding me from some family activity or something.

My mom was too broken herself to help me process my own emotions. So, I learned very quickly to just "suck it up and deal with it." But, sometimes the pain was too much. The only way I knew to stop hurting was to end Renee's life. So, I tried, and failed, four times.

She just kept hurting. I feel bad about that. Her mom even got upset when the school called about it and she let Renee know, real quickly, that her pain, suffering, and even her life, were not important enough to interrupt her workday.

I thought I had convinced Renee that no one would ever really love her and not to believe in love; but, then she got married. I will never understand that. I tried to keep her independent, even while she was married, because people always let you down when you depend on them. She ended up getting let down and hurt just like I told her she would.

Hopefully, she will listen next time she's even thinking about having a relationship.

Renee has become a very strong, successful woman; but I never let her get too confident. I remind her that no matter what she does, it won't be good enough.

I still get pissed off when people hurt her. I lash out and say things before she can stop me. Even her friends say that Renee is "a different person when she is upset." I'm tired of people crapping on us. So, I have started fighting back. I just want to be heard.

If my voice could be heard, I would say:

Leave me alone.

I'm tired.

Why am I not good enough?

What do I have to do for you to love me?

If you loved me, why would you hurt me,
leave me, let others hurt me,
or not help me?

If you loved me, why didn't you tell me or
care about what was happening to me?

I hate you for what you've done to me by
denying me the love I needed.

I have learned that my inner child needs love, rest, reassurance, acknowledgement and mercy. To heal her, I have to be compassionate towards her. I must take care of her mentally, physically, spiritually, and emotionally.

I constantly tell her "you are enough, right now, today without one more college degree and without helping one more person."

I pray every day that my inner child will receive God's grace and stop reading the words that were spray-painted on her soul.

Because they just are not true!

Your inner child
So, how do you heal your inner child?

First, you must take a look at him or her and

identify the emotional wounds that cause you to act the way you do. For example, if you were the peacemaker in your family as a child, you may notice that you do the same thing as an adult. If you were disregarded when you were growing up and your voice was never heard or your opinion didn't matter, you may notice that now, as an adult, you still stay quiet and don't offer your opinion as If it doesn't matter. That's your inner child telling you,

"Don't say anything because your voice won't be heard anyway; it never has been."

Take a look at your relationship and workplace history. Are you the one who avoids conflicts or tries to get everyone to calm down and get along? If so, ask yourself why you do that. Is it because everyone really needs to get along or is it because something inside you gets afraid or anxious when people disagree? What happened in your family when people got angry — divorce, violence, the silent treatment? Do you not use your voice because you still believe you will not be heard? Or do you feel like you are not smart enough to offer an opinion?

Fill in the blanks in this sentence:

When I am in the midst of a conflict, I feel _____ because I am reminded of _____. I believe that the conflict will result in _____.

Realistically, I know that what will most likely happen is

_____
_____
_____.

This is simply an example. **Do this for every characteristic** you identify about your inner child. These may include, but are certainly not limited to things like, afraid, ashamed, unprotected, devalued, betrayed, abandoned, abused, quiet, peacemaker, unloved, parentified (meaning you had to be the parent more than a child); and the list goes on.

Next, you must learn to listen to your inner child and hear what he or she has to say.

Is your inner child angry, hurt, or afraid?

What is your inner child saying?

What is it that your inner child wants the world to hear?

What would help him or her to feel better?

Does he or she need to be heard, to be held or to be acknowledged?

Sit quietly and think about it. What graffiti are you still working to disprove or erase? What are the words you see on the wall of your soul? How do those words make you feel?

Although you were supposed to erase all the negative, untrue graffiti in your last **contemplation** *exercise, I realize that is much easier said than done in your psyche. So, we'll just have to keep erasing any graffiti that pops back up unexpectedly.*

Now, compare the graffiti you are still trying to disprove or erase to the person *you* see in the mirror today. Are those words true? Not, could they be true or were they ever true?

Knowing what you know to be true about yourself, are those words true today?

Finally, spend some time talking to your inner child, telling him/her what he/she needs to hear. It's okay to talk to yourself in this instance. No one will know but us.

If your inner child needs to hear that everything will be okay, tell him that.

If she needs to hear that she is loved, tell her that.

Tell him that you are strong now and can handle life as an adult, even when things are unfair.

Tell her that she is not unattractive or unlovable; but a child of God whose beauty flows from the inside out.

Tell your inner child that no matter what anyone else says (or doesn't say),
you believe in him or her
and you believe that he or she is a wonderful person with a lot to offer this world.

At first, this may feel fake or even uncomfortable. That is normal. Write it down and confess it with your mouth, as a mantra, as often as you need to in order for it to feel more natural — *at least twice a day*.

Ultimately, you must *define "good enough"* for yourself. You must define "good enough" as it relates to your appearance, your career, your accomplishments, your purpose, your thoughts, your feelings, your relationships, and your life.

As long as you are good enough for yourself and your Higher Power, that should carry the most weight. It will take time, though, for you to replace the tape that has been playing in your head and heart all these years. Be patient with yourself, and kind to yourself, as you rediscover who you really are.

Saying good-bye
So, in deciding to change the "tapes" in my head, I had to put my big-girl boots on and say goodbye to my inner child. I do not believe our inner children die; but, we must "fire" them from the job of running our lives. Here is my goodbye letter to my inner child:

Dear Mickey,

Thank you, Little Girl, for being such a fighter. Thank you for caring about how I felt and for not wanting me to hurt. I do not blame you for the suicide attempts; I know you felt like that was the only way to stop the pain. Back then, I actually agreed with you. I am certainly glad we never succeeded, though. I would not have gotten to see you learn to use your voice had we succeeded. We would have left this Earth still feeling unworthy to be loved and feeling as though being perfect wasn't even good enough. What I know today is that none of that is true.

I am a whole, stable adult now, Mickey, and I have to take the reins of my life. I have to face my fears and deal with hurts in order to grow and learn more about myself. I know you like to show people how strong we are by dealing with everything all alone. The truth is, I get tired of being strong all the time. Sometimes, I do want to ask for help. I don't mind being vulnerable, at times, even if that means I will get hurt. God has not always promised me sunshine; but He always sends a rainbow after the rain.

I want you to go play and have fun. Stop sitting on the sidelines; stop being afraid to fail. By whose standards have we been measuring success and failure anyway? By whose definition did we define "good enough?" In my eyes, you were good enough as the kid you were and I am good enough as the woman I am. Success, to me, is knowing that I have lived God's purpose for my life. Failure is not even attempting to do so. Being good enough means being able to look myself in the mirror and know that I have been the best Michael-Renee I can be each day.

Know that I will always love you despite any questionable behaviors. Know that we all make mistakes and that's okay. You are wonderful just as you are. Your feelings are important. Both your joy and your sorrow matter to me.

Love always,
Michael-Renee

Contemplation: What do you want to say to your inner child as you say goodbye? It is time. You must start living your fulfilling, adult life.

Write a goodbye letter to your inner child and let him or her go be a kid.

10 *THE GOOD AND THE BAD*

"There are two primary choices in life: to accept conditions as they exist, or accept the responsibility for changing them." Denis Waitley

Remembering the past helps us not to repeat it. So, remembering what was originally written on our souls, vividly reminds us how far off the mark our parents really were. Once you realize that the words are not true, you can replace them with what is true — what you know to be true about yourself.

There may always be 1% of you that still hears the whispers of the past, especially when you are scared or confused. Remember, that place was comfortable for a long time — it was the only truth you knew. Now, it is time to trust yourself and believe in yourself.

Know that your mother was wrong and prove it —
to yourself.

When you hear the whispers of the past, shut them
down. Recognize them for the distraction they are
and quiet them with the truth. Turn this "stinkin'
thinkin'" into your own positive mantra. Look at
your life in full and count your blessings. Give
yourself credit for what you have added to society.

Self-inventory
It is time to look in the mirror again, take a
comprehensive self-inventory and redefine you.

Who are you?

What is your truth?

Identify the parts of you that are "wonderful" as a
special friend of mine always says – funny,
responsible, compassionate, loyal, driven, etc.
Choose three to five positive words (minimum) that
define you.

What is wonderful about you?

(1) _____ (2) _____

(3) _____ (4) _____

(5) _____

Now, look at the other side — the side that we all

try to deny. Identify the parts of you that are not so great — maybe mean, judgmental, foul-mouthed, selfish, pessimistic, lazy, overweight, etc. We all have good and bad parts; but only when we accept them all do we become whole. Recognize and accept these aspects as a part of you that can be fixed — rather than a part that condemns you.

What needs improvement?

(1) _____ (2) _____

(3) _____ (4) _____

(5) _____

My bad side is named "Michelle." She is judgmental, impatient, and pessimistic. By acknowledging her existence, however, I am able to keep her subdued and remain accountable for my own behavior.

If I am being pessimistic, I know "Michelle" is in control of my thinking. So, I simply dismiss her and allow my rational self to take over.

Denying that "Michelle" exists would mean denying a part of me and relinquishing control of the negative thoughts that she brings. Although, I don't like "Michelle," she is a part of me; and I love me — the whole me — good, bad, and ugly.

No one character trait defines who I am as a

woman.

My mother was wrong. She missed out on a fabulous daughter. She lost years of friendship and bonding. We both missed out on a cherished mother-daughter relationship. Thankfully, however, I wake up every day knowing that I am a good person. I wake up with a goal of being happy, making my family happy, and making a stranger happy with a random act of kindness.

I am a clean, fresh, washable piece of linen that, although stained, brings comfort, warmth, and peace to every person I encounter. I am thankful that God had a purpose for me and required me to fulfill that purpose.

Does that mean that I never doubt myself or that the tapes have stopped playing altogether?

Nope!

I have achieved great success in the United States Air Force Reserve, as a flight nurse veteran of OPERATION ENDURING FREEDOM and currently serving as a mental health nurse at the rank of Major. I have earned a BA in Psychology, a BS in Nursing, an MA in Psychology, and am an ABD Doctoral Candidate for a PsyD in Sport & Performance Psychology at the writing of this book. I have a booming counseling practice and I do what I love to do every day. Yet, there are still days that I may not be happy, may question my value, or may

hear a whisper of "you don't deserve all this."
Then, I have to remind myself that I studied hard
and I worked hard and I deserve whatever successes
with which I am blessed.

I have gotten where I am in life by the grace of
God, by going to *therapy* regularly, and by doing
the required *work* on myself. I am constantly
assessing my position in life and re-evaluating who
I am. If I accept my own definition of "good
enough" for myself, then I need not change
anything. If I identify an area that needs
improvement, or set a new goal for myself to reach,
then I do what's necessary to make changes.

The key to this process is that things change
because *I* want them to change; not because
someone else feels they need to change. **No one
defines me, my life, or my "good enough" except
me.**

Allow no one to define your you, your life, or your
"good enough."

Except you.

> *"Accept responsibility for your life.*
> *Know that it is you who will get you*
> *where you want to go, no one else."*
> Les Brown

Contemplation: So what is your "good enough?" What standards have you set for yourself? What goals have you set? What goals have you accomplished or not accomplished? Why have you or haven't you? How did you beat yourself up for not reaching your goal? I need you to forgive yourself, right now, for failing to meet your goal, for the reason you got held back, for beating yourself up, and for not trying again. Then, make a commitment to yourself that, if you still want to accomplish your goal, you will try again as soon as you have finished this book. How did you celebrate yourself for the goals you did reach? If your answer is: "I didn't do anything [to celebrate];" I need you to plan a celebration for yourself. Take yourself out to dinner, buy yourself a cupcake, pop a bottle of champagne, or something. You deserve it.

Goals for the next 6 months:
1. _____
2. _____
3. _____
Rewards/Celebration:

_____
_____

Goals for the next 12 months:
1. _____
2. _____
3. _____
Rewards/Celebration:

_____
_____

11 *WHO ARE YOU?*

*"He who knows others is wise; he who
knows himself is enlightened."*
Lao-tzu, *Tao te Ching* (sixth century B.C.)

So, where do we go from here? How do we start to
live our lives with a new voice and a new "tape"
playing in our heads?

It starts by defining "you."

Who are *you*?

Your answer is not based on who other people think
you are or say you should be.

Who are you when you are standing naked in front
of your Higher Power?

If you were the only person on Earth, without any
external affirmations, who would you be?

When I introduce myself to new students, at the University at which I teach, I make a clear distinction between *who I am* and *what I do*. Too often, I ask people who they are and the response immediately starts with titles. "I am a mother." "I am a lawyer." And those things are not who we are, they are things that we do — roles that we fulfill. They do not define our inner character, our fundamental beliefs, our joys, and disappointments.

So, again, I ask, *who are you?*

My answer to this question is: I am a whole, intelligent, physically unfit, impatient, emotionally open, spiritually sound, black female who has been to Hell & back more times than most, yet still remains compassionate.

I believe:

God is my Lord and Savior & it is crucial to be obedient to His plan for me

All children should have a voice in the world

Sex is not currency

Love does not conquer all

We must accept all parts of ourselves to be whole

Yesterday is gone; tomorrow is not promised;

today is all we have; so, experience every moment.

I like:

Horseback riding

Watching TLC, Discovery, Discovery Health, & Boomerang

Playing Scrabble

Following the PBR

Writing poetry

Playing board games with my daughter

Bowling

Watching and playing soccer

Learning anything new

Traveling

Belly dancing

I dislike:

Complacency

Lies

Laziness

Abuse of any kind

Disrespectful children

Ungrateful people

Brussel Sprouts

Liver

Now, **the things that I do, include:**

Mom, Grandmom, Sister, daughter, niece, aunt

Friend

Author

Court-Appointed Special Advocate (CASA) Volunteer

College Instructor

Registered Nurse

Doctoral Candidate

Licensed Professional Counselor & Sport Psychologist

Entrepreneur & Business Partner

Air Force Reserve Officer

"Who you are" is defined by the *character traits*
that you feel define your core being (good and bad),
your *fundamental beliefs*, and your *likes and
dislikes*. Our self-definition is fluid and it is honest.
It can change whenever we deem necessary; but
changes are made only when we deem necessary,
not based on external opinion.

We must own who we are and learn to love who we
are for ourselves. If there are things on which we
feel we can improve, then we work on them. By
defining and owning our self-definition, we take full
responsibility for the decisions and choices we
make in life. We cannot blame anyone else when
we fall short; but we also don't have to accept
negative opinions about ourselves when we do.

For example, I am *physically unfit* and, at times,
impatient. These are characteristics that I know are
not good; but they belong to me. I am fully aware
of them and I own my part in them. I could be
physically fit if I put more effort into diet and
exercise. Once I finish my dissertation, I will do
just that. For now, I do as much as I can with the
time I have.

Patience is a trait that I have never had, but work on
continuously. Sometimes I get it right. Sometimes
I get it wrong. I do genuinely try, however, to get

better.

Most important: neither of these traits makes me a bad person.

I do not beat myself up when I don't exercise or I eat some ice cream. I don't get down on myself when I am impatient. I simply recognize my mistake and correct it. If I offend anyone in the process, I make sure to apologize.

> *"Know Thyself"*
> A central component of the philosophy of
> Socrates (469?-399 B.C.)

True power

There is power in knowing who you are. You can get up every morning and know and like the person you see in the mirror. You learn to see your flaws more as challenges than "Scarlet Letters."

By defining yourself, you are empowered to define your own happiness and embrace all of your parts.

My happiness is tangible. I can see it, smell it, taste it, hear it, and feel it. My "happy" is hot pink, smells like fresh baked chocolate chip cookies, tastes like champagne and chocolate covered strawberries, sounds like a whispering wind, and feels like a warm blanket around my heart. I see happiness in the sunset at the beach, in my daughter's smile, in roses, in horses, and in every body of water. I have learned to define my "happy" because I have learned to define me and to embrace every part of me and you can too.

If the words "overweight," "fat," "sloppy," or "obese" have been written on your soul, you can do something about that. Your weight does not define who you are inside. You have the power to either change your weight or begin to love yourself at your current weight; but regardless, the choice is yours.

If the words, "ugly," "stupid," "good for nothing," or "mistake" were written on your soul, you do not have to accept those either. You can change those labels into "beautiful," "smart," "valuable" and "purposeful" by perhaps visiting an image consultant, going back to school, acknowledging what you do for people or your community, or by fulfilling God's purpose for you and your life.

You may also choose to love yourself just the way you are, depending on how you define the adjectives that have been used to describe you. "You are the expert on yourself," as one of my professors, Dr. Gina Hernez-Broome, said once. You have the power to be whomever you want to be — whether people like you or not.

For all the readers of this book, *empowerment* is what I hope you will find for yourselves.

> *"Taking back our power means deciding who we are, and who we wish to be.*

This is only possible when we no longer make our past or other people's opinions 'about us'. " Melanie Tonia Evans

Contemplation: Who are you? It's up to you to define yourself. Fill in the chart to get started. Feel free to make your chart bigger if you need more space to write about how fantastic you are.

Now, define your "happy." If happy was a _____, what _____ would it be/have?
Color? _____
Smell?_____
Taste?_____
Sound? _____
Feel? _____
Where do you feel happiness in your body?
_____
In what things do you see happiness in the universe?_____
_____
_____

Make a collage of images that represent your happiness and put it somewhere where you can always see it to remind yourself that YOU define your happiness each day.

Who I Am vs. What I Do			
Who I Am			What I Do
Character Traits	Likes & Dislikes	Fundamental Beliefs	

12 *NOW THAT THE WALLS HAVE BEEN SCRUBBED*

My hope is that through this book, through my journey, you will find healing and learn to *define yourself for yourself.* I encourage you to *take your power back,* so that external opinions or the lack of external affirmation will no longer break your spirit. Hopefully, you will get to a place where people's opinions of you will no longer be written on your soul as truth; unless it is something that you can honestly own as a facet of who you are.

At no time in life do we ever have to apologize for who we are. We may apologize for insensitive or inappropriate behaviors; but not for who we are at the core. Your self-definition will give you a foundation on which to stand and will keep you from blowing in the wind like a paper napkin. It will become a rock on which to stand up for yourself.

It will guide you in your decision making — what you will and will not do, what you will and will not accept or tolerate.

It will affect how you will allow people to talk to you and to treat you. People will only do to you what you allow them to do to you.

Ultimately, it will help you decide what graffiti gets written on your soul from today forward.

You see, yesterday is gone and tomorrow is not promised; so, today is all we really have. Experience today based on who you have decided you are, not based on the definitions of others.

You may see things a lot differently.

> *"Don't forget to love yourself."*
> Soren Kierkegaard

Final Contemplation: What have you learned on this 100+ page journey? Who are you today after finishing this book? Do you love yourself a little bit more? Were you able to let some stuff go? Were you able to find compassion, forgiveness, or both for your mother (or father)? Have you found hope? I hope, if nothing else, you have found solace in knowing that you are not alone.

Please share this book with others that you think

need healing.

I would love to hear about your experience through this book. Please feel free to share your thoughts and feelings with me via email at michaelrenee@therapywithmichaelrenee.com.

If you are in need of a therapist and don't know where to start:
- You can call your insurance company to get a list
- You can search one of these websites:
  www.psychologytoday.com
  www.goodtherapy.org
  www.therapytribe.com
- You can visit my practice website at www.perfectpeacecc.com and see one of our therapists. We even do distance counseling by videoconference.

References

Stone, D. J. (2009). Parent and child influences on the development of a black-white biracial identity (Doctoral dissertation, Virginia Polytechnic Institute and State University). Retrieved from http://scholar.lib.vt.edu/theses/available/etd-11162009-035955/unrestricted/Stone_DJ_D_2009.pdf

ABOUT THE AUTHOR

Michael-Renee Godfrey is an ABD doctoral candidate, scheduled to receive a PsyD in Sport & Performance Psychology from the University of the Rockies in 2015. Her dissertation is titled *The Lived Experience of Aggression in High School Football Players: A Phenomenological Study*. She is a native Texan with an 18-year-old daughter and a 6-month old granddaughter. She has practiced as an RN since 1999. She is a Major in the U.S. Air Force Reserve & a veteran of OPERATION ENDURING FREEDOM. In 2007, Michael-Renee accepted a spiritual calling to counseling; and opened Perfect Peace Counseling Center, with her best friend from high school, Amani, on September 1, 2010. She is an experiential therapist with a Rogerian theoretical base. She is certified in hypnotherapy and distance-counseling; contemplating working on her certification as a Reiki Master. Michael-Renee also enjoys doing equine assisted psychotherapy (EAP) with her clients & her horse, Hershey. "I am always in awe of how God works as I walk with my clients on their journey to perfect peace."

61015631R00067

Made in the USA
Columbia, SC
21 June 2019